Software

Designer

Alice B. McGinty

the rosen publishing group's
rosen central
new york

To my parents, Saul and Linda Blumenthal

The author would like to thank the following individuals for their valuable contributions to this book: Dave Blumenthal, Christopher Carlson, Mike Clark, Richard Coddington, H. George Friedman, Kevin Maxson, Brendan McGinty, and Robert Walker.

Published in 2000, 2003 by The Rosen Publishing Group, Inc.
29 East 21st Street, New York, NY 10010

Library of Congress Cataloging-in-Publication Data

McGinty, Alice B.
Software Designer / Alice B. McGinty
     p. cm. — (Coolcareers.com)
Includes bibliographical references.
Summary: Explains what software designers do and how to
prepare for a career in software design.
ISBN 0-8239-4086-1 (lib. bdg.)
1. Computer software—Development—Vocational guidance—Juvenile
literature. [1. Computer software industry—Vocational guidance.
2. Vocational guidance.] I. Title. II. Series.
QA76.76.D47 M397 2000
005.1'2'0273 21—dc21

                                                                  99-043239

Manufactured in the United States of America

CONTENTS

ABOUT THIS BOOK

Technology is changing all the time. Just a few years ago, hardly anyone who wasn't a hard-core technogeek had heard of the World Wide Web. Computers and modems were much slower and less powerful. If you said the word "Internet," no one would have any idea what you meant. Hard to imagine, isn't it?

It is also hard to imagine how much more change and growth is possible in the world of technology. People who work in the field are busy imagining, planning, and working toward the future, but even they can't be sure how computers and the Internet will look and function by the time you are ready to start your career. This book is intended to give you an idea of what is out there now so that you can think about what interests you and how to find out more about it.

One thing is clear: Computer-related occupations will continue to increase in number and variety. The demand for qualified workers in these extremely cool fields is increasing all the time. So if you want to get a head start on the competition, or if you just like to fool around with computers, read on!

chapter one

SOFTWARE DESIGN: A BRIEF INTRODUCTION

In recent years, computers have become as essential to our daily lives as indoor plumbing, motor transportation, or electricity. With better technology developing by the day, we're depending more and more on computers to help us pay bills, talk with friends, and type written documents such as this book. Naturally, the demand for the people who program computer software is increasing as well.

Software designers are responsible for creating what is essentially the brain of the computer. Software tells the computer what to do. Every feature from the wording of the welcome note you see when you switch your monitor on to the color of the clock at the corner of your

screen is designed by a software designer. As computer technology improves every day, the need for hard-working and creative software designers increases also.

Before becoming a software designer, though, there are many questions you have to ask yourself. First, and most important, do you like computers? Software designers are around computers all day long. They have to know the technology inside and out, which means long hours of practice.

Second, are you a creative person? Software designers are exactly what their job title describes: They're designers. This means that in many cases you'll be responsible for not only creating how a program works but also how it looks. The color of the features, the font type, the images—these are all elements the designer chooses. Being creative in this business is as important as being knowledgeable.

Finally, are you dedicated? This is a demanding profession. It requires a lot of skill and talent. Many people compare it to being an athlete, such as a baseball or football player, which requires years of practice. Unless you're dedicated, you'll never learn the profession on the expert level. On the other hand, if you prove that you are committed

to the profession, you can do great things.

In reading this book, you'll get a better sense of what it takes to become a software designer and whether or not the job is right for you. We'll go over how software is made, what it takes to become a designer, and career

opportunities in the field. Also, in the back of this book you'll find a list of books and Web sites that you can use as resources for more information on the subject.

A BRIEF HISTORY OF THE COMPUTER ▶▶▶▶▶▶▶

Did you know that the word "calculate" comes from the Latin word *calculus*, which means "a small stone"? In ancient times, shepherds found that putting stones in a pot helped them to keep track of the number of animals in their herds. It was this need to collect and calculate information that led, step by step, to the modern computer.

One of the first machines people invented to help calculate numbers was the abacus. The abacus was invented more than 5,000 years ago in China. It is a series of rods with counting beads that slide in order to keep track of what is being counted. Of course, this instrument can work no faster than human hands can move its beads. In the 1600s, Blaise Pascal invented a machine that used wheels and dials to add numbers. Later, Gottfried Wilhelm Leibniz invented the stepped reckoner. It multiplied, divided, and found square roots.

In the 1700s, Charles Babbage designed a computer-like machine called the analytical engine. It could add, subtract, multiply, and divide. His friend, Countess Ada Byron Lovelace, the daughter of the poet Lord Byron, wrote computer programs for Babbage's machine. The program instructions were in the form of punched cards, an idea borrowed from the French weaver Joseph Jacquard, who used such cards to control the patterns of fabrics produced by his looms. Unfortunately, only a part of Babbage's machine was ever actually built.

The American inventor Herman Hollerith, using the same system of holes punched into cards, built a computerlike machine to add up the 1890 census. You may have heard of the company Hollerith started, International Business Machines, better known as IBM.

The abacus was the first counting machine.

In the 1940s, the world's first electronic computer was invented. The Electronic Numerical Integrator and Computer, or ENIAC, weighed 30 tons (27.2 metric tons) and took up an entire 30-by-50-foot (9-by-15-meter) room. For switching devices, it depended upon thousands of vacuum tubes, which like lightbulbs would frequently burn out. In 1948, scientists at Bell Labs invented tiny switching devices called transistors. These replaced the large vacuum tubes and made computers much smaller. Transistors are made of solid materials and use much smaller electrical currents than vacuum tubes, so they don't burn out, making computers much more reliable.

People soon found many uses for computers. Today computers have revolutionized the way we work and play. New technology continues to make computers smaller and faster, and software has been written to help us in every aspect of our lives.

THE SOFTWARE INDUSTRY TODAY▸▸▸▸▸▸▸▸▸

Today's software industry is huge. To help you understand it, let's break it down into categories. There are two main types of software. The first is systems software. Systems software works behind the scenes to control the basic operations that all computers must perform, such as reading data, controlling the onscreen display of information, organizing the storage of data on the hard drive, moving the cursor when the mouse is moved, and sending data to the printer. The most common examples of systems software

This is the operating software for the Apple Macintosh.

are operating systems such as Microsoft Windows or Macintosh Operating System 10 (OSX).

The second type of software is called applications software. This is the software that you purchase and install on your computer to perform specific tasks. There are many types of applications software.

- Business software: These programs manage big jobs for private companies or governments. They handle accounting, sales, inventory, and payroll records. Sometimes they even control manufacturing processes.
- Educational software: These are programs that teach subjects or tasks, such as reading, math, or science.

- Office software: These are programs that help individuals work productively. Word processors such as Microsoft Word and spreadsheets such as Excel are examples.
- Recreational software: These are the animated computer games that you may already like to play.

Some software is sold in stores, designed for general use by thousands of customers. Other programs are custom-made for people and businesses that need them for highly specialized jobs.

chapter two

HOW SOFTWARE IS MADE

Though there are many different kinds of software, the process of creating it involves the same basic steps. These steps are called the software life cycle. The process begins with an analysis of the problem to be solved.

NEEDS ANALYSIS▶▶▶▶▶▶▶▶▶

The first step is to ask the following questions: Why is this software being created? What must it be able to do? What is the exact nature of the problem to be solved? The software designer must be able to put him- or herself inside the client's head and see the program from the user's point of view.

With custom-made software, the designer works with clients to determine their needs. Mike Clark is the president of Clarkware Consulting. "When I do custom software development," he says, "I take the sketchy 'wants' of the client and create a specification." In a specification, the goals of the software are determined and described.

If the software is to be sold in stores, a marketing plan may be written. The marketing plan tells why the software is needed and who will buy it. It may seem premature to be working on a marketing plan before the software is even written, but by identifying who the customers are, this plan tells the designer a lot about what the software must do and for whom its features must be designed.

Both marketing plans and custom software specifications describe how many workers and how much time and money it will take to develop the software. The client or corporation then looks at the plan. If it approves, the project moves ahead to step two.

DESIGNING THE SOFTWARE▶▶▶▶▶

At the next stage, a software design document is created to show how the software will look and how it will work. "There are usually two parts to a design document," says Clark. "One is for the visual or physical look. The other is for the organization of the code."

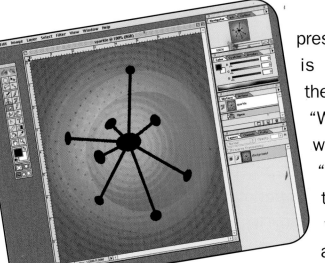

Brendan McGinty, president of Leo Media, is a consultant in the software industry. "When I design software," McGinty says, "I first try to lay out the whole program— what I want it to do and how I want it to work. I like to say that I design the skeleton first and then put the meat on the bones later."

Laying out plans for the text, pictures, and buttons that the user sees and interacts with is known as preparing the user interface design. "Almost every program starts with some kind of splash screen to introduce it," continues McGinty. "Then comes a menu to let you go where you want. Then for each screen, ask yourself what text, picture, sound, music, animation, and video would help to get your message across."

Kevin Maxson, chief technology officer and manager of system development for NovaNET Learning, talks about the importance of design: "In any project that more than one person will work on, the design is really critical. With a good software design document to work from, even junior developers can turn out a quality piece of software."

DEVELOPMENT AND IMPLEMENTATION►►►►►►►►►

During development, the software is put together by programmers following the outline of the design document. Sometimes authoring tools are used to put software together. Authoring tools are programs that allow software to be written by assembling pieces of preprogrammed code like building blocks. Text, pictures, and sound are added to make each program unique.

With more complex programs, much original code is written to tell the computer what to do. Maxson explains, "Once the software design is complete, implementation begins. Code is written, tested, and then reviewed by other developers."

TESTING AND VALIDATION►►►►►►►►►

Once the software is put together, it needs to be tested. Bugs, or mistakes in the program, are found and fixed. Computer programmers spend a great deal of time debugging software, and if the problem is large enough, the designer will also be involved. The software must not only work, but it must also be appealing in design and useful to purchasers.

Dave Blumenthal, a software engineer, talks about the testing stage: "I have to test my code and make sure that it works properly. I also work with others who test the software more rigorously than I can, trying it out on different types of computers."

As Maxson explains, "Once we have a stable piece of software, we verify that it satisfies its goals. Then we pass it through a quality assurance cycle to catch any bugs or performance problems. After that, the software is released."

OPERATIONS AND MAINTENANCE▶▶▶▶▶▶▶▶

If software is to be used over a long period of time, it has to be maintained. The people in charge of it continue to fix bugs that are found in the program. They add new features to the software and then market the revised program as an upgrade. They also improve the software so that it can run on new computers. With the development of faster and more powerful computers, software can perform more complex functions.

chapter three

THE DESIGN TEAM

Sometimes one person completes the software life cycle from beginning to end. More often, though, a team of people work together to create software. In this chapter, you will meet the people on the software team.

THE DESIGN TEAM►►►►►►►►►

"Large projects need many designers," says Mike Clark. "One designer might work with the user interface, which includes fonts, buttons, and screen layout. Another designer might work with transitions between screens, animations, backgrounds, and logos."

Frequently, designers need help from other people. Experts in particular fields, known as content providers, help program designers ensure that the content, or information, in the program is accurate and complete. If the software is an educational program about jungle animals, an expert on those animals may be called upon to provide information for the program.

"One of the greatest bonuses of my job as a software designer is that I get to work in so many different fields," says Clark. "I don't have to be a doctor to work on a cancer treatment program or a children's learning expert to work on a project about museums for kids."

Software designers also work with artists, or graphic designers. "If you aren't an artist, find a good one and have him or her add magic to your program," says Brendan McGinty. Artists help create the special look of a program, and this may affect its ease of use and just how much people like to work with it.

"If the software needs animation, the designer might work with an animation specialist. If it includes video, a videographer could help. These jobs all relate to the project. The software designer may perform some of those jobs or work with someone else who does them," McGinty says.

In educational software, instructional designers are used. Instructional designers have training in education;

many are teachers. They determine the learning objectives, or goals, for the software. They design the software so that it teaches those objectives and then tests it to make sure that the user has learned them.

THE PROGRAMMER▶▶▶▶▶▶▶▶▶

A computer programmer, or developer, puts together the software by writing code or using authoring tools. The programmer translates the designer's plans into specific instructions that the computer can understand and execute.

Writing code can be simple or complex for a programmer. In science, math, and engineering settings, programmers write code to solve problems using complex mathematical formulas. Programs for computer operating systems or animated video games with many levels of play consist of millions of lines of code. A good programmer can organize lengthy sets of instructions so that they not only work but work fast, and so that it is relatively easy to locate bugs when a program doesn't work. Good programming is almost an art form. Two programs written by different individuals may both do the job, but one may work seconds faster than the other because of the superior organization of its code.

In most large projects, teams of programmers each work on only a small segment of the complete program. These sections are called modules or units. The modules are put together later, after each one has been perfected. Much of a programmer's time is spent testing and fixing the program to make sure that it works.

Software designers and developers are sometimes called software engineers. This is most common in science, engineering, and some business settings. Designers who work on systems software, the behind-the-scenes software, are often called systems engineers, systems designers, or architects.

COMBINING DESIGN AND DEVELOPMENT▸▸▸▸▸▸▸▸▸▸

Sometimes software is both designed and developed by one person. The use of authoring tools makes this easy for simple programs. For more complex programs, design and development are done by different people. "Software design and software development can often be done by the same person for small projects," says Clark. "For larger applications, there is just too much work for one person to do."

No matter how many people work on design and implementation, the two steps are always connected. "The programmers keep going into the designer's office asking for clarifications or making suggestions for changes," says Clark.

Dave Blumenthal agrees. "Design and implementation are very closely tied. No software design is perfect on the first pass. As the implementation begins, the design is revised, and missing pieces are filled in."

Some companies prefer to have projects designed and developed by the same person. McGinty states, "I recommend that design and development both be done by the same person so that the message isn't muddled in a handoff to someone else."

HARDWARE ENGINEERS►►►►►►►►►►►

Software designers and developers may confer with hardware engineers. The hardware engineer determines whether the computer can perform the tasks needed to run the software or not. The developer and hardware engineer work together to find the best way for the software's code to communicate with the hardware.

SYSTEMS ANALYSTS►►►►►►►►►►►

Systems analysts look at computer systems as a whole to see what their needs are. Then they determine how to meet those needs. Many times this involves designing special software. Sometimes in custom software development, the software designer does the systems analysis. It is similar to needs analysis, the first step in the software life cycle.

"Every project has a systems analyst, but often the team doesn't realize it," says Clark. "Someone has to step back a little and look at the project as a whole."

OTHER MEMBERS OF THE TEAM►►►►►►►►►

Quality assurance engineers sometimes help test new software to make sure that it functions as designed. Sales and marketing staff promote and sell software. They may also receive feedback from customers and may be able to let the designer know what the customers' needs are.

Once the software is in use, customer support representatives assist people who have trouble using it. Some companies have training departments that offer classes to teach people how to use their software.

These are the people on the software team. Their duties and titles vary depending on the size and type of the project and the company where they work.

chapter four

THE BASICS OF BEING A SOFTWARE DESIGNER

Just as in all professions, software design requires a certain type of person to do the job. Following are what professionals in the field think are important traits software designers should have, not only to get their foot in the door of the industry but also to become successful and be happy with the job.

LOGICAL THINKING▶▶▶▶▶▶▶▶

Are you a clear and logical thinker? If so, you're on your way to becoming a good software designer. In order for designers to bring practical software to the marketplace, they have to have a logical sense of how the program they're designing needs to run. If you were an architect building a house, would you put the kitchen in the attic or the bathroom in the garage? Of course not. In the same way, software designers have to lay out the design of their programs logically. This means making the most important features of the software the most visible and easy to use. It also means making sure that the software is practical and helpful for the end user.

A GOOD EYE FOR DETAIL▸▸▸▸▸▸▸

Have you ever built a house of cards? If so, you know that the tiniest imperfection can bring the house tumbling down and ruin a lot of work. The same goes for building  software. These programs have tens of millions of lines of code with each line depending on the others just like each card in a house of cards supports the others. If there's a mistake in one, the others can be affected. This is why it's important for a software designer to have a good eye for detail. Without this, possibly years, not just hours, of work can be ruined.

PATIENCE

Software developer Chris Carlson says, "I think that one of the hardest lessons to learn in software development is dealing with complexity. Programs can have over one million lines of code—so many that no one person can understand how it all functions." Even if you have a great eye for detail, mistakes will be made. Remember, no one's perfect. So the test of a truly great software designer is not whether you make mistakes, but how you handle them. By staying cool and calm when mistakes occur, you'll have a better chance of succeeding with the project as a whole.

SKILLS

Are you working hard at developing your writing skills? Many software designers are responsible for writing documentation: the notes, handbooks, and instruction manuals explaining how the program works. According to McGinty, "Good writing skills are very important in putting together a piece of software. Make your message interesting and clean."

Are you a good listener? Can you express yourself so that others understand you? Communication skills are extremely important. Designers need to communicate with programmers, artists, and other designers. A designer creating custom software must also communicate with the client.

Carlson says, "A software designer has to listen well to get a complete picture of a client's needs. He or she also has to communicate the ways in which a program will fulfill those needs and, almost more important, what the program cannot be expected to do."

Software designers need good listening skills.

Rob Walker, a Web page developer with Leo Media, agrees. "If a designer cannot communicate his or her ideas or understand the ideas of another person," he says, "valuable production time can be wasted in developing software that doesn't meet the users' needs."

BEING A TEAM PLAYER▶▶▶▶▶▶▶

Do you work well with others? Being able to work as part of a team is also important. "Most commercial programs are so large and complex that they require the teamwork of many designers and programmers," says Carlson. "In order for the parts of the program to work well together, the designers have to work well together."

BEING A STUDENT FOREVER▶▶▶▶▶▶▶▶▶▶

Do you like to learn new things? Software designers study hard to keep up with new technology, because software must work on the newest, most advanced computers. Many times, classes and workshops are offered by hardware and software companies to keep their employees' knowledge up-to-date.

"I work for a start-up company," says Dave Blumenthal. "There aren't enough engineers for everyone to do only what he or she already knows how to do. That means that I'm constantly learning new things."

chapter five

THE JOB MARKET FOR SOFTWARE DESIGNERS

Learning about the field of software design is the first step toward a career in this area. This chapter will tell you how to continue on that path. It covers education, training, and some projects you can try.

JOB REQUIREMENTS▸▸▸▸▸▸▸▸▸

Today, it is easy enough to teach yourself software programming. Degrees from specialized schools are not as important as they were a few years ago. Many employers are focusing more and more on a portfolio of work. If you can show that you know what you're doing, that's one step closer to a career! But even so, formal training is still important and will help you in the long run with your career as a whole.

HIGH SCHOOL TRAINING▶▶▶▶▶▶▶

High schools across the country are realizing how important computers are in daily life. Because kids are becoming more computer literate, schools realize they have to keep up with the times. They're spending more and more money on computer equipment in schools along with hiring qualified teachers to train students how to use them.

Many high schools today offer classes in basic computer skills as well as more advanced courses.

Though computer classes are helpful in getting started on the career path toward software designer, it is also important to take courses in other areas. In

Take advantage of any computer training available in your high school.

software design, you'll not only have to understand how computer programs work but also be able to figure out how the hardware of the computer operates, to visualize the artistic qualities of the program design, and to grasp the basic logic of programming. Therefore, classes in science, math, and the visual arts are important for software designers as well.

FOUR-YEAR COLLEGE DEGREE PROGRAMS►►►

Most four-year colleges offer computer science programs.

Most computer professionals have four-year degrees from a college or university. You will be more marketable if you have one.

A degree in computer science will give you training in the development of both hardware and software. Classes include mathematics, programming, electronics, and artificial intelligence. A degree in computer engineering is similar but concentrates more on electronics. Degrees in information systems focus on systems analysis.

COMBINING AREAS OF EXPERTISE

A great way to be marketable is to combine a knowledge of computers with a second area of expertise. Majoring in computer science with a minor in business would make you a perfect choice for an employer looking for a designer of business software. You could also combine computer science with accounting, the physical sciences, education, or graphic design. It is possible to combine almost any four-year college degree with a specialization in computer science.

TWO-YEAR ASSOCIATE DEGREES▸▸▸

A two-year degree in computer engineering or programming would qualify you for an entry-level programming job. Entry-level programmers, sometimes called technicians, assist software engineers in developing software. They write the actual computer code for portions of programs, and they test software with special equipment. Some junior colleges offer two-year degrees in Web design as well.

GRADUATE DEGREES▸▸▸▸▸▸▸▸

There are several reasons to consider going to graduate school after getting a four-year degree. Many jobs are available for people with advanced degrees. Some are in software research and development labs. You might design software that solves advanced mathematical problems or improves the way computer systems operate. Most of these positions are with large companies.

Graduate degrees also offer the opportunity for one to specialize. Chris Carlson explains, "Because of my interest in computer graphics, I continued on to graduate school so that I could gain an understanding of graphic design. I learned that there are ways of thinking, working, and problem solving that I had gained no inkling of in my engineering education."

INFORMAL TRAINING AND WORK EXPERIENCE▶▶▶▶▶▶▶

Just as important as a college degree is work experience. Employers want to hire designers with experience. How can you get work experience before you land a job? There are plenty of ways!

Play around on computers. Join a computer club. Find a part-time or summer job in the field. Dave Blumenthal suggests, "Projects like Odyssey of the Mind are excellent. Science fairs are good if you're trying to challenge yourself. Puzzles and games are good; designing them is better. Read a lot, too. That usually works."

Spend the day with a software designer. Experience firsthand what he or she does on the job. Ask your school guidance counselor for help making arrangements.

Try to get access to a computer. Mike Clark says, "Experience is the key. Get a part-time job at a computer store. Use whatever computer resources are available at your school or library."

Rob Walker agrees: "I would suggest taking as much time as you can to learn computers—how they work and how they are utilized. This will provide much insight on software design and what users want in their software programs."

"Most important, start programming," says Carlson. He explains why programming experience is important for a designer: "The difference between a software designer and a programmer is like the difference between an architect and a builder. One makes plans; the other carries them out. Certainly, to be a good architect, you have to understand how buildings are built. Similarly, to be a good software designer, you have to understand how programs are built. Practicing programming and developing good programming habits are the best ways to become a good software designer."

PROJECTS TO TRY►►►►►►►►

Carlson suggests, "A good way to learn programming is to look at other people's programs and figure out what they do and why. Experiment by making changes. You can find plenty of example programs on the Web, in programming magazines, or in material that is delivered with the programming environment you use on your computer."

Kevin Maxson suggests, "Figure out some small, interesting programming task, and set out to implement it—even something as simple as a tic-tac-toe game."

"If you want to learn how to program, start with an easy language like BASIC," says Brendan McGinty. "Once you are able to write simple programs using BASIC, move up to [Microsoft] Visual Basic. From there you can learn [Microsoft] Visual C++, and you're on your way. Web page design is pretty easy using tools like Microsoft FrontPage or Macromedia Dreamweaver. Look at cool Web sites, think of some information you want to present, and create something. Try out all of the different things you can do. Play with it."

Clark suggests the following design project: "Find a second person, like yourself, who is interested in software design. Each of you spend one hour writing out an idea for a computer program. Try to write one page about what functions the program should be able to perform (the specification) and one page with drawings showing how the program should look (the visual design). Don't talk to each other about your projects!

"Now trade your work. Pretend you're the programmer who has to implement the program that the other person designed. Did your partner give you enough information about what to do? Does the program use sound, color, or multimedia? What development tools will you use? What happens if the user clicks in different places with the mouse? What happens when he or she quits the program?

"If the designer did a good job, you could actually program what he or she wanted. If this person did a bad job, you might have created a program that wasn't really what the designer wanted or needed and therefore has to be done over."

chapter six

ON THE JOB

With training and experience, you'll be ready to look for a job as a software designer. This chapter will tell you where you might find a job. It describes working conditions and the chances for advancement in the field.

WHERE ARE THE JOBS?▶▶▶▶

Where would you like to work? You will have many choices. Most software jobs are in computer businesses. Jobs in the business setting pay well but can be unstable, since companies may merge, downsize, or go out of business.

Large corporations such as banks, insurance companies, and real estate businesses all employ software designers. Designers with a background in business and accounting create software for personnel and accounting departments. Government agencies such as the military, the space program, and the Social Security Administration all need software designers. School districts, universities, and hospitals employ software designers, too.

YOUR FIRST JOB ▶▶▶▶▶▶▶▶▶

Many people dream of designing computer games like the ones they see in stores. Most of those games are created by large software companies. It is hard to get entry-level design jobs in those companies; most of their designers begin their careers as programmers. After gaining experience and sharing their design ideas, they are promoted into design positions.

It is possible, however, to get an entry-level position designing software for a smaller company. Kevin Maxson says, "Small companies sometimes let developers do their own design. If you are beginning work in a large company like Microsoft or Sun Microsystems, you will probably be implementing somebody else's design work."

CHANCES FOR ADVANCEMENT

Software designers who have worked for many years may advance to management positions, especially if they are good leaders.

Maxson is in a leadership position. "I manage a group of seventeen software engineers and also serve as lead software engineer on many projects," he says. "In my role as lead software engineer, the lion's share of my time is spent reviewing other engineers' work and suggesting solutions to problems."

Development managers, or project leaders, like Maxson coordinate all aspects of a software project. They decide how the software will be designed and developed. They assign tasks to members of the team. Then they supervise the team as it completes the project.

Many experienced software designers start their own consulting companies. Consultants are hired to work on specific projects. When the project is done, the consultant moves on to another job. Consultants are well paid, but, because they must find their own work, their jobs are never stable.

Brendan McGinty shares his experience: "I began my professional career as a software designer/developer. I did my job well and was given the opportunity to manage a small group of other software designers. From there we created software for clients all over the country. We grew our group and made a good reputation for ourselves. After that, I moved up to a higher position that utilized my software design and management skills. That led me to running my own software design and development company."

THE WORKPLACE▶▶▶▶▶▶▶▶

The boom in technology-based businesses in the late 1990s revolutionized the industry. It has been seen as young, hip, and innovative, and the working environment continues to change accordingly.

Where computer software companies used to have stuffy, formal environments, they are now tailored more to the lifestyles of young people, the new generation of designers. An example of how these companies are accommodating this new breed is in their dress codes. Companies

want their employees to be comfortable, so many offices no longer require the traditional suit. Jeans and a comfortable shirt are often appropriate.

To attract new, young employees, many businesses provide laptops and wireless communications, which allow software designers to work from home or while traveling. Whether it is from the comfort of your living room or on a plane to your favorite vacation spot, you can be in touch with the office at all times.

SALARY AND BENEFITS▶▶▶▶▶▶▶

Salaries for software designers have spiked in recent years. Take, for example, the following annual salaries from 1997 compared with those from 2002:

	1997	2002
Computer programming	$35,167	$53,126
Information systems	$34,689	$45,705
Systems analysis and design	$36,261	$45,928
Software design and development	$39,190	$83,294

This recent increase in wages is the result of computer software becoming more and more sophisticated. We're no longer just using software to type term papers. Experts are using the software to make entire movies! Take, for example, the movie *Monsters, Inc.* It was made completely with computers!

EMPLOYMENT FORECAST ▶▶▶▶▶▶▶

Employers will always be looking for talented software designers. More people than ever are using computers, so the demand for new and better software increases every day. Even though there has been a lag in the market for technology jobs ever since the slump in Internet companies in the late 1990s, the market for software will always be around.

As we move into the future, we're beginning to see the industry breaking new ground. In coming years, software will be used outside of computers as well. Right now, devices such as cellular phones, cars, and even television sets all use software. In the future, technology experts believe more and more everyday appliances will be run by computers. Imagine unlocking your front door by touching a pad that recognizes your fingerprint. What would it be like to be able to call up your car from your cellular phone to tell it to start? If any of these technologies ever become reality, it will be because of the designers who helped create the software.

WORDS.COM: GLOSSARY

applications software Software that is used directly by the computer user.

authoring tools Programs that allow a developer to create software without having to program individual lines of code into the computer.

bugs Mistakes in computer programs.

custom software Software that is developed specifically to meet a client's needs as opposed to being sold in stores.

hardware The physical parts of the computer.

software A word for programs or instruction sets that distinguishes them from the hardware or actual computer equipment.

software life cycle The steps followed in the creation of a program.

specification A document stating the goals of a piece of software and defining ways to reach those goals through design.

systems software Behind-the-scenes software that controls the functions of the computer.

transistors Tiny electronic switching devices used inside computers and other electronic devices.

RESOURCES.COM: WEB SITES AND ASSOCIATIONS

Due to the changing nature of Internet links, the Rosen Publishing Group, Inc. has developed an online list of Web sites related to the subject of this book. This site is updated regularly. Please use this link to access the list:

http://www.rosenlinks.com/ccdc/sode

ASSOCIATIONS

Association for Computing Machinery (ACM)
1515 Broadway, 17th Floor
New York, NY 10036
(800) 342-6626
(212) 869-7440
Web site: http://www.acm.org

Information Technology Association of America
1401 Wilson Boulevard, Suite 1100
Arlington, VA 22209
(703) 522-5055
Web site: http://www.itaa.org

Institute for Certification of Computing Professionals (ICCP)
2350 East Devon Avenue, Suite 115
Des Plaines, IL 60018-4610
(800) 843-8227
Web site: http://www.iccp.org

Software & Information Industry Association
1090 Vermont Avenue NW, 6th Floor
Washington, DC 20005
(202) 289-7442
Web site: http://www.spa.org

OTHER RESOURCES

Odyssey of the Mind (OM) Program
c/o Creative Competitions, Inc.
1325 Route 130 South, Suite F
Gloucester City, NJ 08030
(856) 456-7776
Web site: http://www.odysseyofthemind.com

BOOKS.COM: FOR FURTHER READING

Burns, Julie Kling. *Opportunities in Computer Systems Careers*. Lincolnwood, IL: VGM Career Horizons, 1996.

Eberts, Marjorie, and Margaret Gisler. *Careers for Computer Buffs*. Lincolnwood, IL: VGM Career Horizons, 1999.

Goldberg, Jan. *Great Jobs for Computer Science Majors*. Lincolnwood, IL: VGM Career Horizons, 1998.

Stair, Lila B. *Careers in Computers*. Lincolnwood, IL: VGM Career Horizons, 1991.

PERIODICALS

IEEE Transactions on Software Engineering
1730 Massachusetts Avenue NW
Washington, DC 20036
(202) 371-0101
Web site: http://www.computer.org/tse/

Software Magazine
Wiesner Publishing, LLC
7009 South Potomac Street, Suite 200
Englewood, CO 80112
(888) 764-6614
Web site: http://www.softwaremag.com

INDEX

ABOUT THE AUTHOR

Alice B. McGinty is a therapeutic recreation specialist and a freelance writer of children's books. She lives in Urbana, Illinois, with her husband, a software designer, and her two sons.

PHOTO CREDITS